Magnets Are Fun!

Elaine McKinnon

ROSEN
COMMON CORE
READERS

I0792492

Rosen Classroom™

New York

Published in 2014 by The Rosen Publishing Group, Inc.
29 East 21st Street, New York, NY 10010

Book Design: Mickey Harmon

Photo Credits: Cover Schrempp Erich/Photo Researchers/Getty Images; p. 5 Rubberball/Mike Kemp/Getty Images; p. 7 MilanB/Shutterstock.com; p. 9 (magnet) James Steidl/Shutterstock.com; p. 9 (paper clip) magicoven/Shutterstock.com; pp. 9, 22 (wood) Laborant/Shutterstock.com; p. 9 (can) Africa Studio/Shutterstock.com; pp. 11, 22 (background) Awe Inspiring Images/Shutterstock.com; p. 13 iStockphoto/Thinkstock.com; p. 17 (compass) Csaba Peterdi/Shutterstock.com; p. 17 (magnets) monbibi/Shutterstock.com; p. 19 Snowbelle/Shutterstock.com; p. 21 TFoxFoto/Shutterstock.com; p. 22 (glass) Pavlo Loushkin/Shutterstock.com; p. 22 (screw) James Clarke/Shutterstock.com.

ISBN: 978-1-4777-2240-4
6-pack ISBN: 978-1-4777-2241-1

Manufactured in the United States of America

CPSIA Compliance Information: Batch #CS13RC: For further information contact Rosen Publishing, New York, New York at 1-800-237-9932.

Contents

All About Magnets 4

Magnetic Objects 8

North Pole, South Pole 12

Magnets in Our World 16

Big and Small 20

Glossary 23

Index 24

All About Magnets

Have you ever played with a magnet? If you have, you know that magnets pick up paper clips and stick to **metal** doors. Magnets may seem like a mystery, but they're actually pretty simple! Do you know how they work?

Magnets are an example of simple science that can be really cool!

To understand how a magnet works, you have to know what it is. A magnet is a piece of metal that sticks to other metals. But not all metals are magnets. They have to be made of magnetic metals. Iron, nickel, and cobalt are magnetic metals.

Magnets can be made by us or they can be found in nature. They're all made of metal.

iron

Magnetic Objects

Magnets can only pick up objects that have magnetic metals in them. That's why magnets can't hold wood or glass. Sometimes, something looks like it's magnetic, but it's not. One example is a soda can. A can is made of metal, but it doesn't contain iron.

Soda cans are made of a metal called aluminum. Aluminum is not magnetic.

All magnets have a magnetic field. A magnetic field fills the area that surrounds a magnet. Some magnetic fields are strong. Others are weak. A magnet with a powerful magnetic field can **attract** things from far away. A magnet with a weak magnetic field can only pick up things that are very close.

Size doesn't affect a magnet's magnetic field! Some small magnets can be strong, and some big magnets can be weak.

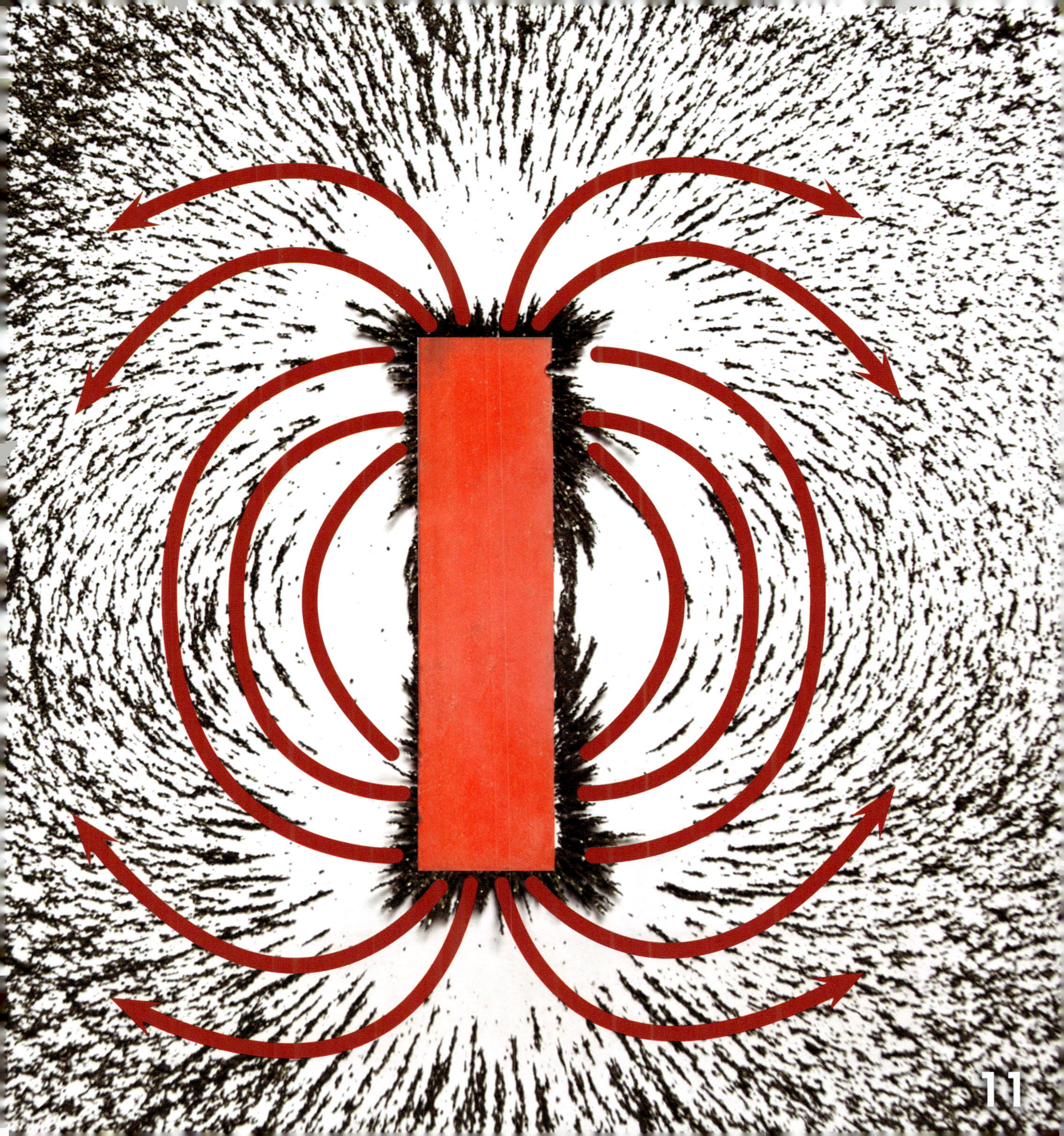

North Pole, South Pole

Every magnet has two poles. One end of a magnet is the north pole. The other is the south pole. A magnet's poles are created by **atoms**. Atoms have **electrical charges**. Atoms with the same charge go to the same pole. When you use a magnet, the charged atoms at the poles are what objects stick to.

Atoms can have either a positive charge or negative charge. Some atoms don't have any charge at all.

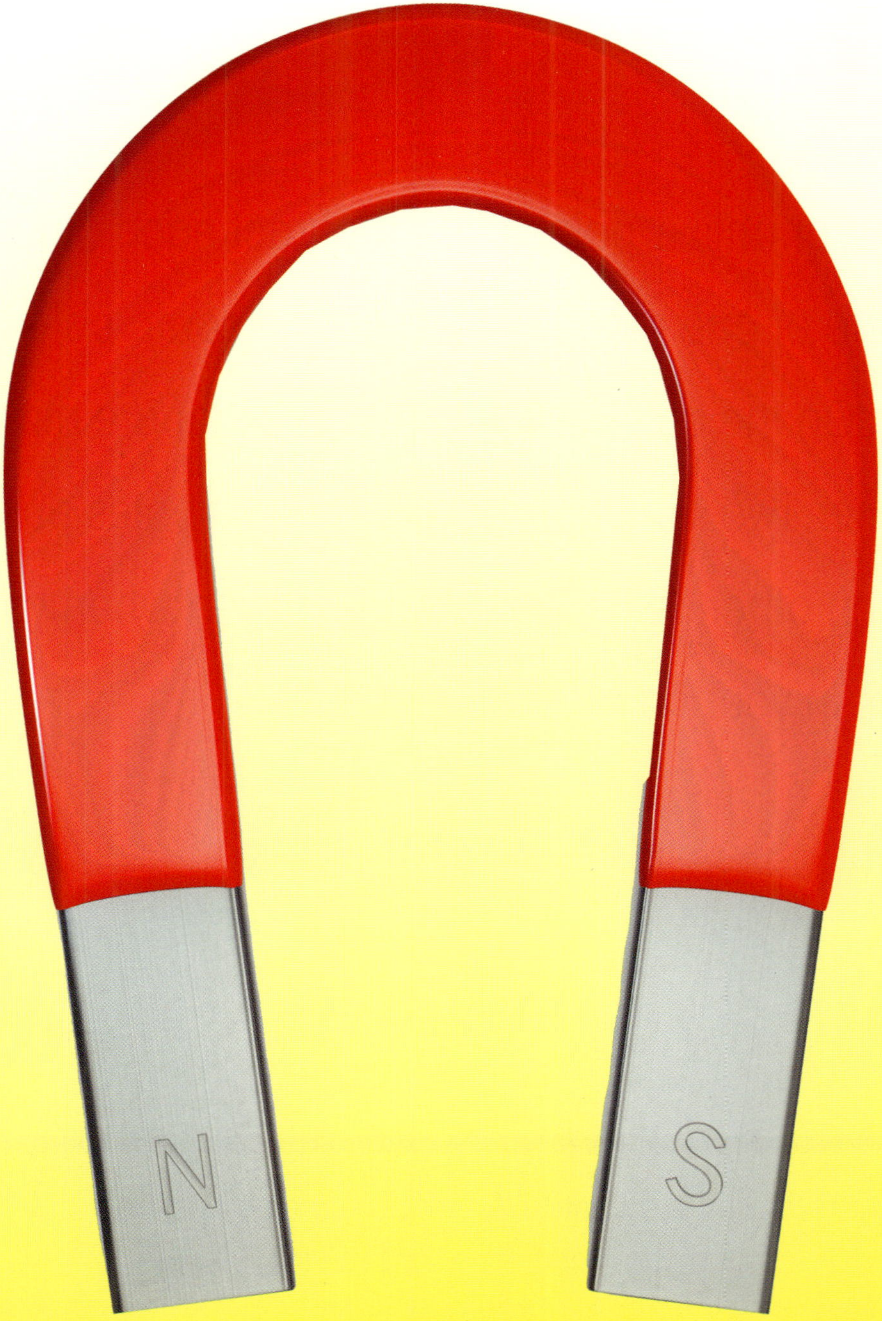
N
S

Opposite, or unlike, poles always attract each other. The north pole of one magnet sticks to the south pole of another. On the other hand, two poles that are alike **repel** each other. Two north poles or two south poles push away from each other. You can feel this happen when you hold magnets in your hand!

You can never make two of the same poles stick,
no matter how hard you try!

S
N
S
N

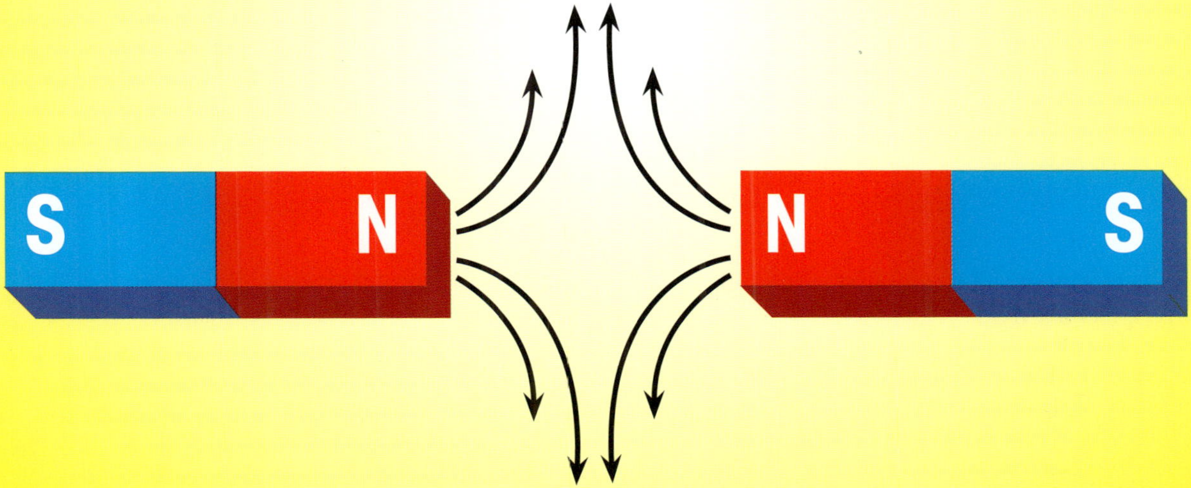
S
N
N
S

Magnets in Our World

Can you think of where you use magnets in real life? You might have magnets stuck to your refrigerator. The magnet attracts the steel refrigerator door through the pictures you hang up. Some computers and toys have magnets in them, too. Magnets are everywhere!

Can you think of anything in your house that has or uses a magnet?

280
300
320
340
260
240
20
40
W
NW
N
NE
S
E

Did you know that Earth is a magnet? It's a magnet because its **core** is made of iron. We use Earth's magnetic poles when we use a **compass**. Earth's poles attract a compass's magnetic needle. Then, the compass tells us where north is.

Earth has a strong magnetic field. We can't feel it, but it reaches all the way into space.

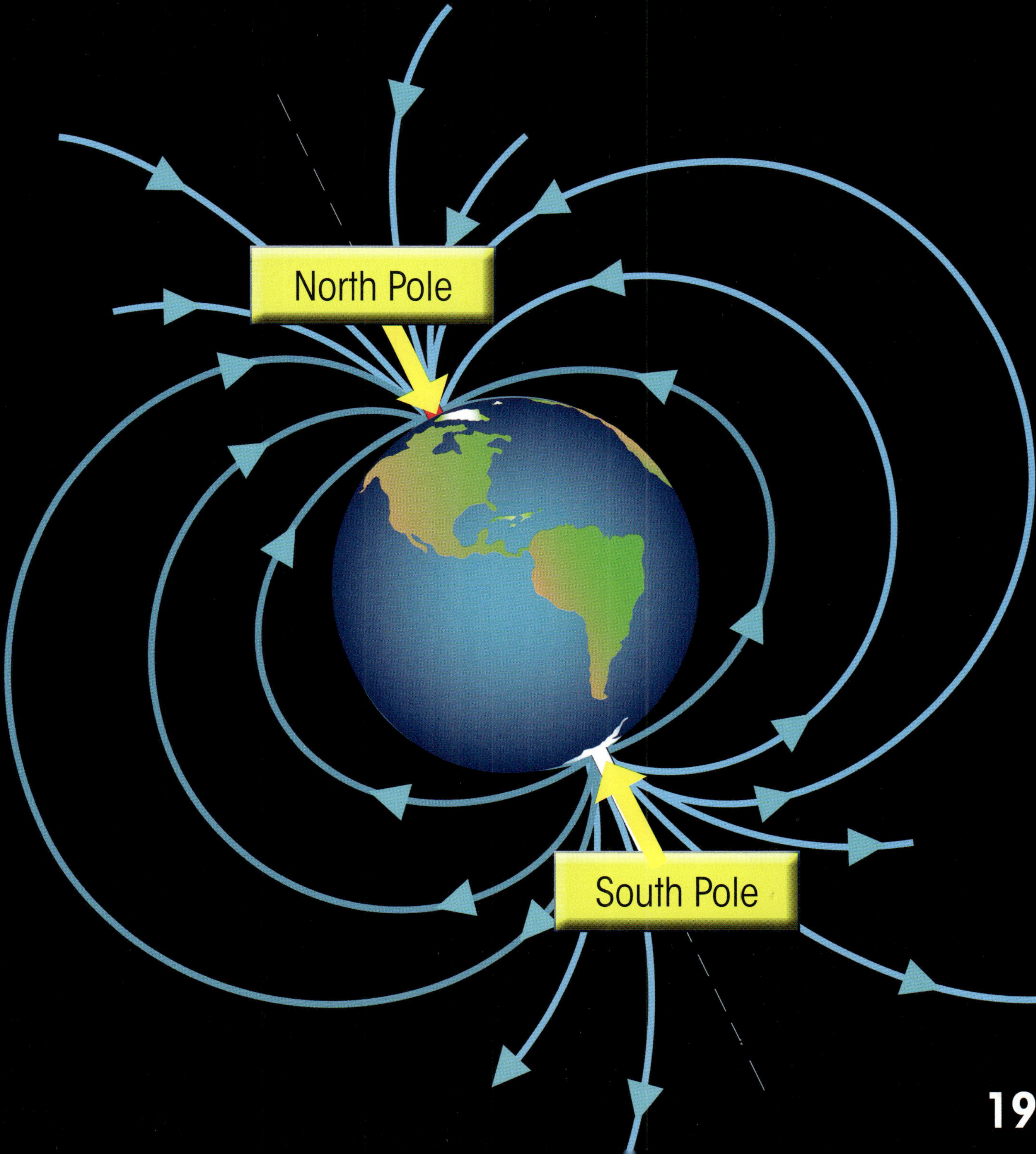
North Pole
South Pole

Big and Small

Magnets can be big or small. Large magnets are used in tools and big machines. Tiny magnets help our computers and toys work. No matter how giant or little, all magnets are fun! Have you ever used a magnet?

What are some examples of big magnets?
What are examples of small magnets?

Is It Magnetic?

object	magnetic?
 glass	no
 iron	yes
 wood	no

Glossary

atom (A-tuhm) A tiny bit of matter. Everything that exists is made of atoms.

attract (uh-TRAKT) To pull toward.

compass (KUHM-puhs) A tool that shows directions. The needle of a compass always points north.

core (KOHR) The center of something.

electrical charge (ih-LEHK-trih-kuhl CHARJ) The amount of electricity in an object. It can be positive, negative, or zero.

metal (MEH-tuhl) Shiny and hard matter.

repel (rih-PEHL) To push away.

Index

aluminum, 8
atoms, 12
attract(s), 10, 14, 16
cobalt, 6
compass, 18
core, 18
Earth, 18
electrical charges, 12
iron, 6, 8, 18, 22
machines, 20
magnetic field(s), 10, 18
metal(s), 4, 6, 8
nickel, 6
pole(s), 12, 14, 18
repel, 14
steel, 16